W9-CEJ-753

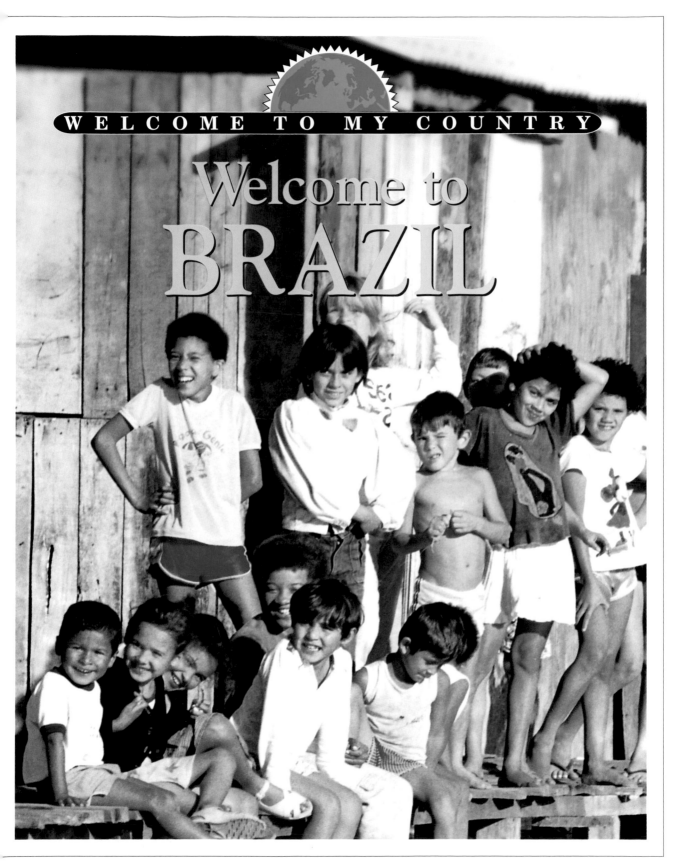

WELCOME TO MY COUNTRY

Welcome to
BRAZIL

Gareth Stevens Publishing
MILWAUKEE

Written by
NICOLE FRANK/LESLIE JERMYN

Designed by
HASNAH MOHD ESA

Picture research by
SUSAN JANE MANUEL

First published in North America in 2000 by
Gareth Stevens Publishing
1555 North RiverCenter Drive, Suite 201
Milwaukee, Wisconsin 53212 USA

For a free color catalog describing
Gareth Stevens' list of high-quality books
and multimedia programs, call
1-800-542-2595 (USA) or
1-800-461-9120 (CANADA).
Gareth Stevens Publishing's
Fax: (414) 225-0377.

© **TIMES EDITIONS PTE LTD 2000**
Originated and designed by
Times Editions Pte Ltd
Times Centre, 1 New Industrial Road
Singapore 536196
http://www.timesone.com.sg/te

Library of Congress Cataloging-in-Publication Data
Frank, Nicole.
Welcome to Brazil / Nicole Frank and Leslie Jermyn.
p.   cm. -- (Welcome to my country)
Includes bibliographical references and index.
Summary: An overview of the history, geography, government,
economy, people, and culture of the South American country, Brazil.
ISBN 0-8368-2493-8 (lib. bdg.)
1. Brazil--Juvenile literature. [1. Brazil.]
I. Title. II. Series. III. Jermyn, Leslie.
F2508.F66   2000
98121--dc21   99-042436

Printed in Malaysia

1 2 3 4 5 6 7 8 9 04 03 02 01 00

PICTURE CREDITS
A.N.A. Press Agency: 3 (center), 19 (top),
   20 (top)
Bes Stock: 7 (bottom)
Bruce Coleman Collection: 7 (top), 9, 13, 40
Contexto: 2, 14 (all), 15 (top), 34
Focus Team Photo Agency: 26 (both), 27
Haga Library Inc.: 12 (top), 43, 45
Jeremy Horner: 8
The Hutchison Library: 21, 36
Björn Klingwall: 16, 31, 32
John Maier, Jr.: 5
Eugene G. Schulz: 41
Still Pictures: 3 (bottom), 4, 17, 18,
   19 (bottom), 22, 23, 24, 39
Liba Taylor Photography: 35
Topham Picturepoint: Cover, 1, 6,
   12 (bottom), 15 (bottom), 20 (bottom),
   25, 29, 30, 38
Trip Photographic Library: 3 (top), 28,
   33, 37
Vision Photo Agency Pte Ltd: 10 (both),
   11 (both)

Digital Scanning by Superskill Graphics Pte Ltd

Contents

Words that appear in the glossary are printed in **boldface** type the first time they occur in the text.

Welcome to Brazil!

Brazil is the largest country in South America and the fifth largest in the world. A long time ago, kings and queens ruled Brazil. Today, people of many different races and cultures make up Brazilian society. Let's get to know the people, lifestyle, and culture of Brazil!

Opposite: Water skiing, swimming, and boating are all popular pastimes at Brazilian beaches.

Below: About 160 million people live in Brazil, which has the largest population in South America.

The Flag of Brazil

Brazil's flag is green with a yellow diamond in the center. Inside the diamond is a blue globe with stars and a banner. Each star represents a state. The star above the banner represents Brasília, the capital.

The Land

Covering an area of 3,286,487 square miles (8,512,001 square kilometers), Brazil is larger than the United States. Ten countries border Brazil on the

north, south, and west, while its eastern coast faces the Atlantic Ocean. Brazil can be divided into five geographical regions: north, northeast, south, southeast, and central-west. Each region has unique characteristics.

The north is Brazil's largest region, but few people live there. The huge Amazon River basin stretches east to west, from the Andes to the Atlantic.

Above: The Amazon River cuts through the rain forests of Manaus.

The northeast region is the poorest part of Brazil. It is marked by three types of landscapes — the coast, the *agreste* (ah-GRAYSH-tay) higher up, and the **sertão** (sayr-TAO), or highlands.

Over two-fifths of all Brazilians live in the southeast, where the cities of São Paulo and Rio de Janeiro lie. Gold is mined in Minas Gerais.

Left: The city of Rio de Janeiro lies in front of Sugar Loaf Mountain.

South and Central-West

The south is a small region with only three states. The central-west boasts the capital, Brasília; the Pantanal (the world's largest swamp); and part of the Amazon River basin.

Above: A rainbow adds to the beauty of Iguaçu Falls.

Climate

Most of Brazil is tropical — the temperatures stay warm all year round. The south experiences distinct hot and cold seasons. Sometimes, it snows in the mountains. The central-west region has a dry season and a rainy season.

Wildlife of All Kinds

Brazil's natural habitats — rivers, deserts, grasslands, and forests — support many species of wildlife. About 10 percent of all the plants and animals in the world live in the Amazon basin! Many of its plants, fish, and insects still await discovery.

Below: Jaguars in the Pantanal get ready to fight.

History

Two to five million native Indians were living in Brazil in the sixteenth century when the Portuguese arrived. The Portuguese established sugarcane plantations and employed native Indian workers. When disease killed many Indians, however, Africans were shipped to Brazil as slaves. These slaves worked just on the plantations

Above: West Africans were brought to Brazil as slaves.

at first. Later, they also worked in gold mines and as domestic servants for the Portuguese. As mining declined, coffee exports grew. Slaves worked on the plantations until slavery was abolished in 1888.

Above, left: Pedro I took power in 1822.

Above, right: Pedro II ruled Brazil with his daughter, Isabel, until 1889.

Independence

In 1822, Brazil won independence from Portugal. Pedro I became king. His son, Pedro II, ruled until 1889, when the people rebelled and overthrew him.

Opposite: African slaves were often ill-treated and punished.

Left: Juscelino Kubitschek ordered the construction of the modern city of Brasília in the 1950s.

The Twentieth Century

The rich controlled Brazil's government until the 1920s, when others began to demand changes. In 1930, rebel leader Getúlio Vargas came to power. He helped Brazil **industrialize**. His **successor**, Juscelino Kubitschek, encouraged foreign companies to do business in Brazil.

In 1964, the military ended the presidency of João Goulart and started a dictatorship that lasted more than twenty years.

Below: President Juscelino Kubitschek held office from 1956 to 1960.

Economic Developments

Above: Brazilian workers chop wood to make roofs.

Brazil's economy grew quickly, but in 1973, a major **recession** hit the country. Brazil ran up high debts, and political **corruption** became a problem. In 1993, finance minister Fernando Henrique Cardoso introduced a plan to save the economy. With the success of his "Plan Real," Cardoso became president. Today, Brazil is part of Mercosur, a trading group that also includes Argentina, Paraguay, and Uruguay.

Pedro Álvares Cabral (1467–1520)

Cabral is considered the founder of modern Brazil. He led the Portuguese expedition that arrived in Brazil in 1500. After that, many Portuguese went to Brazil to set up plantations and settlements.

Pedro Álvares Cabral

Henrique Dias (?–1662)

Dias, a man of African descent, fought for the Portuguese against the Dutch in Brazil. He won many honors during his army career. In 1656, the Portuguese granted Dias the right to free the slaves in his unit. After that, all black militia units were called "henriques," in his honor.

Henrique Dias

José Joaquim da Silva Xavier (1748–1792)

Silva Xavier fought for Brazil's independence from Portugal and was executed as a rebel in 1792. Brazilians regard him as a hero of the nation.

José Joaquim da Silva Xavier

Princess Isabel (1846–1921)

The daughter of Pedro II, Isabel helped her father rule Brazil. She put laws into effect that ended slavery. In 1889, the monarchy fell. Isabel lived the rest of her life in **exile** in France.

Above: In 1888, Princess Isabel passed a law that freed all slaves in Brazil.

Getúlio Vargas (1883–1954)

Vargas was president of Brazil for eighteen years. He made many contributions to the economy, health, and education. During his second term, he was accused of corruption. Instead of resigning, Vargas committed suicide.

Left: Vargas says his goodbyes to Brazilian pilots fighting in World War II.

Government and the Economy

The **federal republic** of Brazil consists of twenty-six states and one Federal District, Brasília. The country is ruled by a president, a vice-president, and a Congress. The president appoints cabinet ministers to help him. The Congress is divided into two houses — an 81-member Senate and a 513-member Chamber of Deputies.

Below: The Palace of Justice is located in Brasília, which is also home to the Federal Supreme Court. Brazil has many regional federal, military, and labor courts.

Left: Voting is not **compulsory** for Brazilians aged below sixteen or above seventy, but the law requires all those aged between eighteen and seventy to vote.

The Judiciary

Two supreme courts and several types of regional courts help enforce law and order in Brazil. Each state and the Federal District also have a governor and a system of laws.

Elections

All Brazilians aged sixteen and above have the right to vote. The current president of Brazil, elected in 1994, is Fernando Henrique Cardoso.

Above: Sugarcane workers travel by horse cart.

Resources and Agriculture

Brazil is a land of many natural resources. A large number of factories and businesses center on resources, such as metals, gems, and wood.

Brazil produces large amounts of cotton, sugar, coffee, and other goods. Rice, nuts, wheat, and corn are also grown. Some of these crops are exported, or sold to other countries, around the world.

Trade

Brazil imports large amounts of food, oil, coal, chemicals, and fertilizers from other countries. Tobacco, sugar, coffee, iron, leather goods, and paper make up some of its biggest exports.

Brazil enjoys prosperous trade with the United States, Germany, Japan, and Italy. As a member of Mercosur, Brazil also trades with other South American member countries — Argentina, Paraguay, and Uruguay.

Above: A worker extracts gold. Brazil has a strong metal-mining industry.

Left: A lab researcher studies malaria. About one-third of the 65 million workers in Brazil are women.

People and Lifestyle

Ethnic Groups

Many different **ethnic groups** form Brazil's population. These include native Indians, Africans, and Europeans (mostly Portuguese). *Mamelucos* (mah-may-LOO-kohs) are of mixed Indian and Portuguese descent. *Cafusos* (cah-FOO-sohs) are of mixed Indian and African descent. People of mixed African and European

Above: Brazil's Amazonian Indian population is shrinking as the country modernizes.

Left: Elementary-school students take a break from their lessons.

descent are called *Mulatos* (moo-LAH-tohs). Recently, many Europeans and Japanese have settled in Brazil.

Above: Many blacks and Mulatos live on Brazil's northeastern coast.

Class Differences

Skin color and income are generally closely related in Brazil. Whites tend to be richer than darker-skinned people. Poverty affects about 70 percent of Brazilians. In Rio de Janeiro, there are about two thousand homeless children.

Going to School

The educational system in Brazil lacks funding. Although primary education is required through eighth grade, many children from poor homes must end their education early and go to work. Most schools in the countryside do not even offer all eight grades. Mainly the middle and upper economic classes can afford to send their children to secondary school. Only the very rich can afford a university education.

Above: Students wait for classes to begin.

Health

Brazil's public health care system is also poorly funded. Only the rich can afford to be treated at hospitals and clinics. In northeastern Brazil, two out of every three homes do not have running water. Living conditions are often dirty and crowded. Many babies die from disease or **infection** soon after birth.

Left: The priority for most people in poverty-stricken areas is food.

23

Close-Knit Families

Brazilians value family ties. A household often includes the grandparents or married children. Family members who do not live together usually visit one another often and meet for Sunday lunches.

Below: Brazilian family members remain close throughout their lives.

Sometimes, big Brazilian families get even bigger — when parents ask two other adults to be their child's godparents or when a family informally "adopts" a child from a poorer home.

Children

Children grow up with a strong sense of family. At a young age, they learn to interact with adults, brothers and sisters, and cousins. Even after they marry, some continue to live with one set of parents or the other.

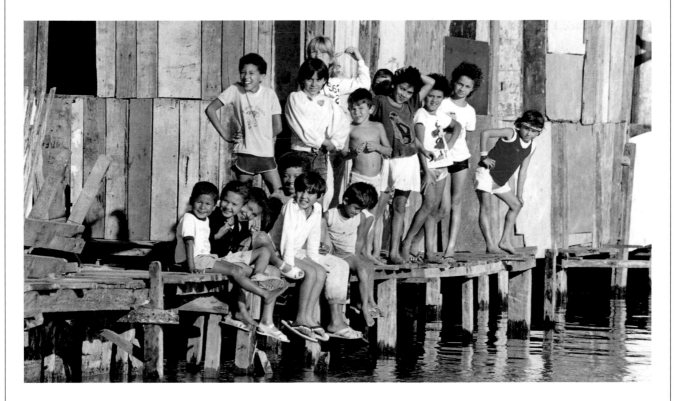

Men and Women

Men and women play different roles in Brazilian society. Women are expected to stay home and look after the children, while men work to support the family.

Above: Brazilian children pose for a picture.

Religion

Brazil is home to the largest number of Catholics in the world. Although most Brazilians are Catholic, they also believe in many **supernatural** forces outside of the Catholic faith. Many religious practices combine Catholic and African customs and beliefs.

Below: Icons of the Catholic faith.

Other Beliefs

Carrancas (kahr-RAN-kahs) are carvings of monsters attached to boats to scare away evil spirits in the water. They are no longer used today, but eyes are similarly painted on boats to guard against underwater dangers.

Members of the Valley of the Dawn **cult** believe many people will die in the new millennium, but that cult members will survive. Their temple is in Brasília.

Below: People take part in a **candomblé** (cahn-DOM-blay) ceremony. Candomblé is a religion that combines West African and Catholic beliefs.

Language

Brazilian Portuguese

Brazil's official language is Portuguese, but it differs from the Portuguese spoken in Portugal. Without European influence, Brazilian Portuguese developed separately through the nineteenth century, with its own accents and expressions. People from different parts of Brazil speak the language differently.

Below: Brazilian Portuguese includes words from African and native Indian languages.

Left: Many Brazilian children love to read.

Cordels and More

Brazilian themes, such as slavery, the Amazon River, and city life **dominate** local fiction.

Cordels (COR-dayls) are story-filled **pamphlets** featuring heroes and local events. *Cordel* means "cord" and refers to how the pamphlets are sold strung up on strings in shops. In the northeastern countryside, singers perform the stories of the cordels to eager audiences.

Arts

Aleijandinho, Brazil's first renowned sculptor, carved religious figures in wood. Modern artist Mário Cravo creates sculptures using concrete.

Left: Bruno Giorgi's *Two Warriors* sculpture stands in Brasília.

Heitor Villa-Lobos (1887–1959)

Composer Heitor Villa-Lobos was born in Rio. In Paris in 1927, he performed his musical compositions. The performance was so successful that he became world famous.

Theater

Before World War II, only the wealthy in big cities could afford to attend plays. Since the 1940s, however, new theater groups and performing techniques have reached wider audiences.

Above: This opera house is located in Manaus. Brazil's oldest theater is in Minas Gerais. It was built in the early eighteenth century.

Architecture

Europeans brought the **baroque** style of architecture to Brazil in the sixteenth and seventeenth centuries. Brazilians added local touches to the style.

The next big event in architecture was the construction of the capital, Brasília. Architects Lúcio Costa and Oscar Niemeyer designed and built the modern city in 1956. It is still an architectural wonder today.

Above: Brasília's cathedral was designed by architect Lúcio Costa and his student, Oscar Niemeyer. They used open spaces, curves, and **geometric** shapes in their designs.

Arts and Crafts

Certain regions in Brazil are famous for their crafts. Indians of the northern Amazon make jewelry, weapons, and musical instruments. Artists in Minas Gerais produce many useful objects from soapstone, agate, and quartz. The northeast features beautiful clothing and lace. *Marajoara* (mah-rah-joh-AHR-ah), a special pottery, comes from Marajó Island.

Below: Soapstone carvings are made in Minas Gerais.

Leisure

Brazilian cities offer plenty of places to have fun and keep fit. Urban Brazilians enjoy shopping, dining out, and going to sports and dance clubs. The beach is another great attraction.

Left: Brazilians have fun at the beach, but windsurfing is a luxury many cannot afford.

Time to Relax

Brazilians relax in front of the television. They especially love *telenovelas* (tay-lay-noh-VAY-lahs), or evening soap operas with dramatic plots and interesting characters.

Brazilians spend many pleasant evenings chatting away at home or in bars or cafés. They also enjoy friendly debates about political issues.

Soccer

Brazil is truly a soccer-mad country! Boys begin playing the sport at a young age. Soccer clubs encourage people to become members, and crowds fill the stadiums at professional matches.

Brazil's national team has won the World Cup four times — 1958, 1962, 1970, and 1994. Brazilian Pelé, the "King of Soccer," is one of the greatest players of all time.

Above: When big soccer games take place, many businesses close for the day because their workers are watching the match.

Kickboxing and Other Sports

Capoeira (kah-poh-EYR-ah), or musical kickboxing, is a sport unique to Brazil. Slaves, who were not allowed to fight, developed the sport. Since capoeira looks as much like dancing as fighting, the slaves were able to practice their fighting skills in secret.

Brazil's athletes excel at many other sports, including auto racing and tennis. Volleyball and basketball are also popular.

Below: Two girls practice capoeira, a kickboxing sport performed to music.

Reasons to Celebrate!

On January 1, New Year's Day, a boat procession carries a statue of Lord Jesus of Seafarers along the Salvador coast. People say that sailors who participate in the festival will never drown.

Left: Two boys take part in a parade on Independence Day.

José Joaquim da Silva Xavier, or Tiradentes, fought bravely for Brazil's independence from European control. He was executed in 1792. Brazilians remember him on April 21, Tiradentes Day, with music and contests.

Below: At the beach, small boats are filled with flowers and set afloat as an offering to Iemanjá, Queen of the Seas.

September 7 marks Brazil's Independence Day. On this day in 1822, Pedro I declared Brazil's independence.

Food

Brazil's national dish is ***feijoada*** (fay-zhoh-AH-dah), a delicious combination of various meats, black beans, onions, and garlic. Feijoada is served with rice, vegetables, and fried **manioc flour**. The national drink is *caipirinha* (kye-peer-EEN-yah), a mixture of sugarcane alcohol, lime, and sugar.

Below: A Brazilian man toasts manioc flour. The flour is served with feijoada and many other dishes.

Eating in Brazil

Brazilians eat a small breakfast. Lunch is the biggest meal of the day, and, whenever they can, Brazilians eat lunch at home as a family. Dinner is served between 7 and 9 p.m.

In Brazil, good table manners are a sign of politeness and good behavior. Food is generally eaten with a knife and fork and hardly ever touched with the fingers. If you approach a Brazilian who is eating, he or she will always offer to share the meal with you.

A B C D

1

N

State Boundary
Tropic of Capricorn
National Capital
City
River
State Capitals

VENEZUELA

GUYANA

SURINAME

FRENCH GUIANA

COLOMBIA

AMAPÁ

RORAIMA

Eq

Amazon

MARAJÓ
ISLAND

2

♦ **Manaus**

Amazon

AMAZONAS

PARÁ

MARANHÃO

CEARÁ

RIO GRANDE
NORTE

Roosevelt

PARAÍBA

Olinda

ACRE

PIAUÍ

PERNAMBUCO

RONDÔNIA

ALAGOAS

3

PERU

TOCANTINS

SERGIPE

MATO GROSSO

BAHIA

♦**Salvador**

São Francisco

ANDES MOUNTAINS

Federal District
(Distrito Federal)

BOLIVIA

■ **BRASÍLIA**

Pantanal

GOIÁS

MINAS GERAIS

ESPÍRITO
SANTO

MATO GROSSO
DO SUL

Paraná

SÃO PAULO

4

PACIFIC
OCEAN

PARAGUAY

**Rio de
Janeiro**

RIO DE JANEIRO

ANDES MOUNTAINS

Paraná

♦ ▲ Sugar Loaf Mountain

CHILE

**São
Paulo**

PARANÁ

Tropic of Cap.

*Iguaçu
Falls*

SANTA CATARINA

ATLANTIC OCEAN

ARGENTINA

RIO GRANDE
DO SUL

5

URUGUAY

BRAZIL

Above: Many people head to the beach for a day of sun and fun!

Acre A3
Alagoas D3
Amapá C2
Amazon River
    A2-C2
Amazonas A2
Andes Mountains
    A3–A5
Argentina B5
Atlantic Ocean
    D4-D5

Bahia D3–D4
Brasília C4

Ceará D2–D3
Colombia A1–A2

Distrito Federal C4

Espírito Santo D4

Goiás C3–C4

Iguaçu Falls B4

Manaus B2
Marajó Island C2
Maranhão C2–C3
Mato Grosso B3–C3
Mato Grosso do Sul
    B4–C4
Minas Gerais C4–D4

Olinda D3

Pantanal B4
Pará C2–C3
Paraguay B4–B5
Paraíba D3
Paraná C4–C5
Pernambuco D3
Piauí C3–D3

Rio de Janeiro
    (city) C4
Rio de Janeiro
    (state) D4
Rio Grande do
    Norte D2–D3
Rio Grande do Sul
    B5–C5
Rondônia B3
Roraima B2

Salvador D3
Santa Catarina C5
São Paulo (city) C4
São Paulo (state) C4
Sergipe D3
Sugar Loaf
    Mountain D4

Tocantins C3

Uruguay B5

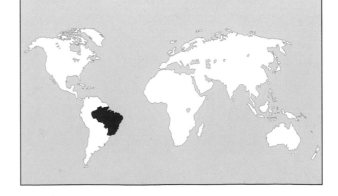

Quick Facts

Official Name	República Federativa do Brasil, Federative Republic of Brazil
Capital	Brasília
Official Language	Portuguese
Population	160 million (1998 estimate)
Land Area	3,286,487 square miles (8,512,001 sq. km)
States	Acre, Alagoas, Amapá, Amazonas, Bahia, Brasília (located in the Federal District), Ceará, Espírito Santo, Goiás, Maranhão, Mato Grosso, Mato Grosso do Sul, Minas Gerais, Pará, Paraíba, Paraná, Pernambuco, Piauí, Rio de Janeiro, Río Grande do Norte, Rio Grande do Sul, Rondônia, Roraima, Santa Catarina, São Paulo, Sergipe, Tocantins
Highest Point	Pico de Neblina 9,888 feet (3,014 meters)
Major River	Amazon River
National Anthem	"Ouviram do Ipiranga as margens plácidas" "From Peaceful Ipiranga's Banks Rang Out a Cry"
Currency	Brazilian real (2.04 real = U.S. $1 in 1999)

Opposite: A blaze of color at the Carnival celebrations in Rio.

Glossary

baroque: a style of art and architecture of the early seventeenth to mid-eighteenth centuries. The style features complex, flowery designs.

Cafusos (cah-FOO-sohs)**:** people of mixed African and Indian descent.

candomblé (cahn-DOM-blay)**:** a religion that combines West African and Catholic beliefs.

compulsory: required by law.

corruption: the result of dishonesty.

cult: a system of religious worship marked by certain group ceremonies and rites.

dominate: to make up the majority.

ethnic groups: people sharing common cultures, religions, and languages.

exile: the state of being forced to leave a country and not allowed to return.

federal republic: a nation in which power is held by the people, who elect representatives that form a central government.

feijoada (fay-zhoh-AH-dah)**:** the Brazilian national dish, made with black beans and several types of meat.

geometric: marked by lines, angles, and shapes.

icons: pictures or images of religious figures, such as Jesus Christ.

industrialize: to build factories and general businesses on a large scale.

infection: the effect of germs on untreated wounds.

Mamelucos (mah-may-LOO-kohs)**:** people of mixed European and native Indian descent.

manioc flour: a nutritious starch from the root of the manioc plant.

marajoara (mah-rah-joh-AHR-ah)**:** a special type of pottery from the island of Marajó.

Mulatos (moo-LAH-tohs)**:** people of mixed African and European descent.

pamphlets: small, unbound sheets.

recession: a period when production, employment, and earnings fall below normal levels.

sertão (sayr-TAO)**:** the Brazilian highland area inland from the Atlantic coast.

successor: a person who replaces or takes over from someone else in a position of authority.

supernatural: objects or events that cannot be explained by the laws of nature or science.

More Books to Read

The Amazon. Great Rivers series. Michael Pollard (Benchmark)

Amazonia. Ends of the Earth series. Susan Powell and Rose Inserra (Heinemann)

Brazil. Country Insights series. Marion Morrison (Raintree/Steck-Vaughn)

Brazil. Economically Developing Countries series. Anna Lewington and Edward Parker (Thomson Learning)

Brazil. Festivals of the World series. Susan McKay (Gareth Stevens)

Brazil. Major World Nations series. Evelyn Bender (Chelsea House)

Brazil: An Awakening Giant. Discovering Our Heritage series. Mark L. Carpenter (Dillon Press)

Carnival. World of Holidays series. Catherine Chambers (Raintree/ Steck-Vaughn)

Rio de Janeiro. Cities of the World series. Deborah Kent (Children's Press)

Yanomani: People of the Amazon. David M. Schwartz (Lothrop Lee & Shepard)

Videos

Amazon: Land of the Flooded Forest. (National Geographic)

Brazil. (Lonely Planet)

Brazil. (New Video Group)

Brazil — Rio de Janeiro. (Education 2000)

Web Sites

www.odci.gov/cia/publications/ factbook/br.html

www.sci.mus.mn.us/greatestplaces/ book_pages/iguazu2.htm

darkwing.uoregon.edu/~sergiok/ brculture.html

www.vivabrazil.com/

Due to the dynamic nature of the Internet, some web sites stay current longer than others. To find additional web sites, use a reliable search engine with one or more of the following keywords to help you locate information on Brazil. Keywords: *Amazon, Bahia, Carnival, Pelé, Rio de Janeiro, samba, São Paulo, soccer.*

Index